TRUMPED

(FEAR & LOATHING ON THE TRAIL TO POWER or

HOW I LEARNED TO LOVE FOX NEWS)

BY

Anthony Edward DeFiore

"There is no such thing as bad publicity,

And a sucker is born every day!"

P. T. Barnum

The TRUMP National Doral Golf Club

looked like a postcard from your Aunt who fled to Florida for

the sunshine and bugs as the thief came through her front

window. "IT'S CALLED THE **TRUMP** DORAL NATIONAL

GOLF CLUB, YOU FUCKING IDIOT!..... YOU'RE FIRED!"

yelled that voice that killed a thousand checking accounts. The

poor man in long sleeves, long khaki pants and a hat fit for a

bee keeper just smiled. The voice from Hell continued, "YOU,

YOU, YOU FUCKING WETBACK! GET THE FUCK OFF THIS

GOLF COURSE!" The man in overalls just kept smiling. The

entourage surrounding the great fire breather was in stoned

and petrified silence as they squirmed in their Gucci shoes and

Prada designs. They were hand-picked clothing for them to

wear by the dragon himself. Why not?! They were his kids. He

could dress them anyway his money could buy. The

groundskeeper just kept smiling. And the anger seethed

through the makeup, false tan spray paint and toupee of orange... of course being the new Black. It reminded his kids of the great inferno and volcano that they had been forced to adapt to over their four decades of his tortuous narcissistic rage. The pay was always good. But the hours were hellacious, especially when Dad went into a fit. And we were about to see one of those in a minute. "AND IT IS NOT A GOD DAMN HAIR PIECE YOU JACKASS!" was his common refrain.

Just then a five year old cherub dressed like Lord Fauntroy scampered towards the legs of his grandfather. Such a genial scene. Such unencumbered love. His mother was shuttering in fear! What would be the punishment if her child did something wrong? Anything. The terror of suspense froze her into silence. It always does. The lad kept running up to his grandpa.

"Don, Don!" the little boy roared in perfect form! The instructions from his tutors demanded him to call his grandfather by his proper moniker: "Don, Don"

The little angel squawked triumphantly, "Don, Don, that silly man can't speak English like me! Right "Don, Don"!?" The Lion seemed to melt in his alligator shoes as he grabbed for the little tyke at his knee. "Yes, little one, now don't slobber on my slacks." The little guy froze. It is that easy to break a kid. It's an emotional hijack of the Amygdala that engenders the fight, flight or freeze response for life. It tormented the "Don, Don" that his children all behaved the same way. The Freeze. Look in their eyes sometimes. And now his grandson froze as well.

His frozen family killed The "Don, Don" in rage! It's called Narcissistic Rage! But God does have his plan for ameliorating narcissists and sociopaths a like. The next generation of these monsters usually sells paper flowers in

Vermont or has a bike shop in Santa Monica if only to flee the rage of the "Don, Don". But for a quick moment the "Don, Don" thought to himself. The little dwarf was right. The grease ball Mexican couldn't speak English (The man was actually Cuban), but The "Don, Don" thinks they are all Mexicans because that's all they tell him on Fox). The kid was right! It made sense. But The "Don, Don" s adrenal glands were tingling. His rage was still palpable. He counteracted the logic with demeaning glee and the power of control! "FUCK HIM! FIRE HIM ANYHOW! HOW DARE HE NOT SPEAK ENGLISH AND WORK FOR ME?"

The poor immigrant from Cuba without papers, who floated to Key West in a dingy, was still smiling. He was escorted off the premises of THE TRUMP DORAL GOLF COURSE, and he was happy. Of course he was. Why? Well, first, he won his bet. He lasted for the longest duration of any employee in the betting pool which started the previous week. Second, he was double dipping now! And third, he'd be working in two minutes across the street parking cars for $5 more an hour then the "Don, Don" was ever paying him. These immigrants to America have been hustling to make it and on their way to the American Dream by working their asses off at any job. They have been doing it for 500 years. Except the African Americans. They were the only people who came to America in chains, of course, and that is only if you don't count the "Don, Don" s wives from eastern wherever. They knew how to behave through stupidity or avarice take your pick. A dollar is a dollar. So, as the little boy cried his way to his mommy and tears fell on her skirt, his grandfather cringed and made a face of contempt. "I'LL MAKE A MAN OUT OF HIM IF IT KILLS ME!" he thought to himself. I'll make him my protégé thought The "Don, Don" and then yelled, "RIGHT BOYS!" His four sons knew exactly his thoughts as any good codependent would. They stood in utter icy fear and loathing. None of them could budge.

~

THE FEARSOME FOURSOME

The "Don, Don" stood at the first tee

waiting for his ball to be washed for him. The girl never wavered.
"Don, Don" was in ecstasy. She had such great form. No little
breasts. And she stroked his ball so well. "Here you go sir!" the
young vixen smiled and bobbled next to her boss. "Thank you
my precious little one. I have big plans for you," he exclaimed to
her. It was The "Don, Don" s contribution to the Women's
Movement. His ball gleamed in the summer sun like a freshly
polished apple, or a rosebud if you please.

The gold ball looked so large in the palm of his hand. The
"Don, Don" thought to himself. Then he realized it. He really did
have small hands. It caused him to feel insecurity. And
inferiority. And low self-esteem. He seemed to cringe and fight
the beast within him that tormented him every waking moment
of his entire life and made him work, and work and work and

strive and build bigger and bigger and bigger and..... Well you

know why... Small things do that to some.

Richard Nixon guided his every move in life next to his

Daddy Dearest. But it was Nixon also who told him to see a

shrink like The Trick had done most of his adult life. It only

helped Nixon after Watergate. Before that, Nixon's Inner Self

was lost in Whittier, California somewhere. Poor bastard was

brilliant, but he was so tormented.

There he was. The "Don, Don". He stood as master of all

he surveyed on the 1st Tee at Doral! "Great! It's great! Like

America! Well, more like Me!" he exclaimed silently to himself.

He followed up, "I truly am!" He had updated his slogan from

"Have Fun!" as his casinos lay in ruins at the Jersey Shore. They

were unable to keep up with the much stronger casinos on the

Brigantine Bay. Those newer casino types appealed to the young

millennials who The "Don, Don" never really got and neither did his kids ~ who were actually millennials. Wealth has a way of excluding you from the rest of your peers when you love to live better than they do all the time and are locked into a Faustian timeshare with your Dad....

Even the snakes and alligators surrounding The "Don, Don" on the 1st tee were mystified. The serpent wouldn't even offer him fruit from the tree of knowledge knowing full well that The "Don, Don" would decline to eat from it because he already believed that he owned the tree which was situated at the 13th hole. "Amazing," he spoke, "I truly am!" He slithered, "Sweetheart, wash me another ball will you beautiful?"

"Ohhhh hehehehe," the buxom blonde giggled and bounced noticeable to the golf ball washer next to The "Don, Don". She stroked it up and down gently, but even she never could guess why it was so small."

This man of means was a master of the universe via Great Neck and rental properties that housed most of the pornographic industry in Manhattan for decades. He was Daddy's little helper until he helped himself too much to the help. That was tenants' whooooo.....wares, and he was then whisked away by Daddy Dearest to military school. There he suffered from the harshest of brutality and bullying known to mankind. The making of sociopaths by our pseudo elite private school academy system. They are the patrons of near wealth. It is as if it were some kind of WASP Communion or Religion. Oh, how the disease of narcissism, pseudo wealth and devouring capitalism propagates its species and fucks up the planet daily. The 1% of the 1% usually has a long road of genetic refuse in its cleansing and wealth maintenance process. The "Don, Don" and his family were tossed off that bus early in their orientation to this process. In fact, they had what is known amongst the American Calvinist Elite as "Loud money". It was worse than "New Money" to the Pilgrims. It really wasn't a great deal of wealth in elite circles, but to the television viewers and those watching brainwashed, it was a shit load of money! So, The "Don, Don" was headed to a life of privilege via the small screen and small focused camera shot. Charlie Steiner said it best, "Trump first wanted to be on the back page of The New York Post. So he bought a USFL team. Then he wanted to migrate to Page Six. And after that, he wanted the cover of the New York Post." Folks, that's all it is in a nutshell.

As for his wealth, in Rockefeller terms is was not that much in the game of the really rich. But he was determined to make a splash with his money in life because let's face it, in The "Don, Don" s life, like all sociopaths, he deserved it. And he was entitled to it. His name would be affixed on to everything from New York to New Guinea! Even his favorite jelly doughnuts would have his name baked on to them which if he might say, "Are really good, if I must say so myself."

The Sociopath. The Narcissist. They are terms thrown around like confetti these days. The disease of self-centered ego reliance has been slammed pretty well from 2008. No more High School Principals driving Maserati(s) and having a pool in their 8 bedroom three garage home in the cookie cutter developments in the sticks. No, it was back to the duplexes for those "teachers". But to The "Don, Don", his road to the disease of Sociopathy was paved from the womb. It sometimes can be genetic I believe. He was the wretched off spring of both Daddy Dearest and Mommy Dearest. The kid didn't have the chance. At least The Kennedys and The Hyde Park Roosevelts have some kind of empathy for people due to their Catholicism or the plague of disease that attacked FDR or the traumas that hit both of their families like accidental death. But to the truly Sociopathic John D. Rockefeller Sr. or Frick, Pulitzer or Hearst, your children are just your tools of your own self-aggrandizement and augmentation of your ego. Basically, they only exist for your bragging. "Don, Don" s older brother did not survive the rigors of the sociopathic reign of his parents. Although, wealthy and privileged beyond the other 99%, The "Don, Don" s first born brother carried the weight on his shoulders of the truly sick, demented and child slave-driving sociopaths that he shared a bedroom with on Park Avenue. That was about the extent of the love shown to the first born in this family. And this first born with a truly loving heart died a slow death of Percocet, valium and the like until his brain was mush and the hospital machines kept him alive. The children of sociopaths who either have a loving heart or The Love of God in them are tortured by the sociopathic parent devils in their lives. And they never really live long or prosper in peace. God gets them outta here long before the true decimation descends upon them from below. Only certain Romans and off spring of "The Gods" can survive the initial carnage of their lives from the sociopathy that bore them, but these parents too are beaten down mercilessly as both their sin and reality knows no mercy on themselves from within. They are truly the enemies within themselves. They lay prone and diseased in a dark room with a ventilator on full blast when they die. And nobody gives a shit about them except for their money.

~

The man approaching the 1st tee was a legend not only in his own mind but in the world. You can't look at him and not smile. Just like Willie Mays. Oh, he has his haters, but they'd love to have him in their political party any day. Just lock up the women!

The stroll was obvious. The gait all his own. The cigar was Cuban. And the accent was still Southern Draw. He smoked the best and why not? He was The 40 something President of The United States. Except for World's Heavyweight Champion, there's no better Title to have. Except "Dad" of course.

Mr. 40 something was looking a bit haggard these days. He didn't seem to be himself. Very thin, not as vibrant. Looked like cancer to most or a failing ticker. Can't take a guy off quarter pounders and French fries cold turkey and expect him to look good. That stuff gets the heart pumping baby! Just use olive oil instead of butter, and you'll live forever. But our fine fellow was sporting a Doral cap and didn't know olive oil to butter to short ribs which he knew very, very well hailing from Arkansas. But that was a looooooong time ago. He looked Southern, talked Southern, could eat Southern and knew how to throw the Yankees under the bus better than Big Papi. All things considered he represented the image of a Southern President but never forget, his offices were at the top of the park. Central Park that is. NYC. And that's in Harlem my friend. You can eat at Sylvia's and pretend you are diverse like Bill O'Reilly, but when this man walks Malcom X Boulevard, HE IS HARLEM! He's bigger than Bumpy Johnson was or Sugar Ray Robinson. Well, maybe not Sugar Ray. LOL. But he was The First Black President in American History, and it wasn't Barack Obama. It was this guy, and he's as white as snow, even his hair.

~

They'd been here before. The "Don, Don" and the "Prez." Hell, they were good buddies. The Prez, The "Don, Don" and their better halves, albeit The "Don, Don" had many wives and mistresses, knew each very, very well. The Prez was very faithful these days. He only played the field and hard numbers at the casino. The other easy numbers hardened his arties a bit to say the least. And you know, those women weren't even that attractive. Folks, if I'm tossing away my career, I'm hitting Marilyn Monroe. I'm not hitting the hair dresser! Whatever. If it's the other guy standing there, it's going to be the Best, Terrific, Amazing, and he knows that very well, believe me...... YIKES!

"Excuse me, Mr. President....," politely spoke The "Don, Don". He could kiss royal ass if he needed something, and was well versed at it from kissing his Dad's ass. He was rather adroit also at being bent over at military schools and by his first wife. His first wife being the person who holds the death nail to this sociopathic bastard any time she wants to drop the hammer. Why do you think he keeps all the kids surrounding him everywhere? They're there to fulfill his need for hostages to protect him from the knowledge of his first wife. Maybe number two? Number three wouldn't know a speech from a beach.

Beetch. Bitch? Your call. But ain't it nice to see justice always come out in the end. God will not be mocked, and he answers prayers. As for marriage number 2, well let's just say, the hookers lost out to hope and not experience. She was an absolute G & G match up. Costs a lot of money for a little trim either way you look at it. Just say'in.

The Prez stood on the first tee puffing away on his cigar, and you could see life nearly come back into his haggard face. I'm betting if we got this guy on an Ageless Male regimen, some Cubans and we got him some Quarter Pounders regularly, he'd be in tip top form.

The Prez just winked. The hottie blondie blushed. The "Don, Don" was jealous. When aren't these sociopaths jealous? They'd steal crumbs from an ant. It's not like Jimmy Breslin said that mobsters and politicians can't find anything too small not worth stealing. They just want to feather their nests because they can get wacked or voted out in a heartbeat. And where would their families be? No, these sociopaths steal on a subconscious compulsion that is fit for an embarrassing hard on.

      As the boys puffed and huffed, the conversation turned to politics. "So Mr. President, are you going to make an admirable First Lady?" The "Don, Don" ridiculed and raised his chin and nose in that wannabe haughty style fit for only pseudo Blue Bloods and Brahmins. He was seething that The Prez was trying to screw his secretary! "SHE WILL ONLY WASH MY BALLS!" The "Don, Don" silently announced and screaming at The Prez all in one orange colored flip of the comb over! The Prez just laughed. "Ha! Ha! My friend! I ain't falling for that one. Hell, I didn't even bring my blue pills! And believe me, life is so much more relaxing when you can regulate the steam with those blue pills." The "Don, Don" seemed slighted, "HOW DARE HE DEFY MY SARCASM AND MANIPULATIVE MEGLOMANIA!" The "Don, Don" remained silent with his lip puckered and ascending into the clouds and ready to rage! "Anyhow, my better half will be hear in a heartbeat. I'll have to dump the Cuban soon!" said The Prez. The "Don, Don" just sat in obscure silence on the bench next to the tee and livid at being deep-sixed by the ultimate philanderer. What The "Don, Don" didn't know was that he was also a worthy and mutual sociopath opponent. The Prez just opened up a drawer and compartmentalized The "Don, Don" in one motion. All that Monica stuff taught him well. ;) The young assistant just stood there or better yet hung their like she was a piece of beef for all they gave a shit.

Just then, the leaves rustled... and the ground shook! She had arrived! それはゴジラです！ Even The "Don, Don" bristled. But he kept his style and grace by leaning on his driver (which was really his three wood, but he had it relabeled as a Driver so he could brag about his golfing prowess). These sociopaths know no deception not to be used to manipulate people .... Or public opinion.

[Oh, The Japanese translation is "IT IS GODZILLA!"]

She rumbled along! This woman could trounce elephants if she had too. The ground shook and did shimmy! Like your average 500 pound offensive lineman moving forward, but with a nimble skip. And this women still had a little shake left in her own shimmy. And The Prez always had the hots for her because of it. Marriage is sometimes the match of completely, unbelievably, perfectly matched and bizarre coupling like a Ferrari and a minivan racing through the streets of Monaco! And that Ferrari and Van had nothing on these two. It was love at first ballot. They knew they were going to the White House one day. So did The "Don, Don". At least The "Don, Don" said he did... for a while anyhow.

Her fiery gaze could freeze you in your shoes. She was completely determined every minute, and her eyes had seen a great deal of trauma. Isn't it always like that. They mesmerize you with those wild and laser beam eyes, but deep down they are marshmallow. The "Don, Don" was like that too. He was a little scared boy deep down. But his marshmallow was "smored" out a long time ago and fell into the campfire when his military school fraternity brothers tied him up to a tree and put the largest pine cones up his ass for sport. Yes it's sick and disgusting and how could someone write like this, but then again, how perverse do you have to be to speak like Donald Trump does these days. The PTSD starts somewhere. But for Godzilla, it started on the porch steps in Scwwwwwanton, PA.

The Prez went white.... er! He exclaimed, "OH SHIT!" and with those words he tossed his cigar as far as his double play flip to second base could fly. It floated by The "Don, Don" and nearly hit his secretary. She yelped and danced and jiggled, and the two men ogled her breasts dancing in her thin white blouse. They looked at each other and smiled. The Hottie smiled flirtingly back at them. For a moment you know the two perverts were thinking threesome. I don't know what it is, but in politics, I saw most people screw around with everyone they could like they were stray cats in heat. No couth, and no decorum. No class; just ass. Made me sick and to be honest, how do these freaks get as far as they do? The answer is sociopathy and it ain't a lie. But damn! Can they do it with the best of them. I just watched a Big City Mayor on MSNBC proclaim all of his Liberal bona fides, and I tell you as Jesus Christ is in Heaven I heard this prick use the "N" word like molasses flowing off a bee's ass all his life. They lie with such alacrity and dexterity that the truth never gets in their way, and these one eyed people are the kings in the land of the blind ~ washed. I get sick....

The Cuban laid on the grass. No, it wasn't the landscaper that The "Don, Don" fired in Chapter One. No, it was the cigar. "I SAW THAT YOU TWO!!!!" yelled the First Lady. She was ready to kill The Prez! At the moment, The "Don, Don" was just another campaign check to her. She knew him well. The three of them were "best friends" in The Big Apple! Wined, Dined, Golfed, and talked politics like all great Liberal Scions do in the finest halls, banquet roof tops, penthouses and suites from The Upper East Side, The Plaza to Wall Street and beyond. Three Liberal Peas in a pod. That's right, The "Don, Don" was a Category 5 Liberal Democrat. He was all about Abortion Rights, The Social Welfare State, Separation of Church and State. You see all Sociopaths are like that. For one reason, it gives them more power. Less people, placated entrepreneurial drive and No "god" greater than The "Don, Don". It works like a charm! So many cameras hit The Prez and The First Lady over the years that The "Don, Don" loved to bask in the warmth of their glow. It feed his narcissistic supply needs to a hilt. Adulation, Praise, Unfettered Love and Admiration is like sun light and water to grass. It grows wildly and fast. And the narcissist / sociopath needs it constantly to survive. Like a Vampire on Blood. That's why these guys are called Emotional Vampires. They will suck you dry for their own avaricious aims and then dump you on the side of the road like a dead carcass when they are done. It is absolutely nihilistic.

~

The Prez was being put on notice. "I TOLD YOU TO STOP SMOKING THOSE, DICKHEAD!" The First Lady roared with derision. The cigar laid on the ground. Like a prime rib falling off its plate onto the floor. If it's only there a few seconds, it's still edible. 5 seconds and its trash. A cigar can lay on the ground for years, and you can still try to smoke it. Watch those old hobos on the rails of America trying it. Better yet, we have a million homeless or near homeless people in our country. Look out the window.....

The silence hung in the air with the smell of honeysuckle, cut grass and manure fertilizer. A lethal smell of golf. However, for The Prez and The First Lady, the final Armageddon was to commence... again!

The Prez and The "Don, Don" were caught. The Prez knew from past experiences that a cigar in the wrong place could get his ass in hugeeeeeeeeeeee trouble. The young buxom blonde went bug eyed. The First Lady closed in like a sky filled with B-29s over Dresden. The noise and fear were deafening. And nobody was saying a word. But The "Don, Don" would save the day as he always did among his sycophants... They were trained seals in his world... or so he thinks.

The "Don, Don" and The Blonde knew that he held her career job and future career in his little hands... literally. Oh she washed balls for him all right, and he rewarded her with a start to her climb up the corporate ladder. Like he was Roger Ailes on that blue pill. The Blonde followed The "Don, Don" s eyes. It was like he had mental telepathy control on her. She froze like a robot. She knew what to do. She was a trained seal.

The Blondie leaned down. The Prez couldn't help but to look down at her and her cleavage. The "Don, Don" laughed at him because now he had the sexual conquest over him! The Prez wouldn't be the first one to have her. Sociopaths always count petty victories... down to the penny.

And at that precise moment, The Hottie picked up the Cuban and took a puff of it. She nearly turned green! But, she seemed to have some practice with holding the torpedo Monte Cristo #2. Fine dexterity with the rod. And she held the cigar as if she smoked them all her life. The First Lady yelled at them all! "ARE YOU SHITTING ME!?"

The Prez thought he was cornered! He yelped out, "No sweetheart... It's hers...." The First Lady screamed, "SHUT UP YOU LYING ASS!" She was born in Scwwwanton, PA to a coal miner family, and she could speak like a Molly Maguire any time she wanted too!

The First Lady said, "You are going to tell me that this beautiful young woman is going to be smoking a cigar in that slinky outfit on a golf course?!" The Prez retorted in his best

Maxwell Smart, "Would you believe....."

"DIDN'T I TELL YOU TO SHUT UP, JACKASS?" The

First Lady buried him. She, who had been down this road before

with him and with great embarrassment and disgust, wasn't

about to leave it go by any small measure! "OK!" she spoke, "You

want to blow up your heart, get cancer and throw your legacy and

my political future to the dump heap of history ~ you go right

ahead Mister!" She snarled out her sociopathic preoccupations

and delusions of grandeur in the blink of an eye. They are so deft

with motive and a lie. Like a lion constantly looking at a gazelle.

The "Don, Don" roared his approval in his heart. He loved wild

game steaks.

The "Don, Don" sensed an opening. He could now swoop

in, save the greatest political marriage in US History (Save FDR

& Eleanor) and maybe get that Federal Land he desired to build more in South Florida. Always the scheming bastard. Can you see why they win a lot? Like a Queen Bee Teenager manipulating the entire high school. But the stakes here are the nuclear codes not lunch money. Makes you shudder to think about it...

But The Blonde Bombshell took her commands from The "Don, Don" like R2D2, and she proceeded to speak the exact words The "Don, Don" was thinking. Amazing! But every codependent knows, you can hear their voice in your head after a sociopath gets a chance to train you for a while. The Beauty lied to The First Lady like a champ. The First Chick retorted, "Sweetie, you do know I've dealt with lying dip shits like you before in my life and especially with numb nuts over there." The Blondie smiled knowingly and just nodded her head in approval. The Prez dropped his eyes and lip like a puppy. The "Don, Don" roared, "SEE! All good! Come on my friends, let's have fun golfing! My wonderful executive assistant would never lie to you my dear First Lady." He gave the First Lady a hug, and she seemed to melt into his shoulder like butter. Deep down they are all softies. The Prez smiled. He thought, "Boy, I wish I knew how to do that?!?" Sociopathic jealousy again. They are relentless. The Prez moved to the tee to hit his ball. The "Don, Don" smiled at The First Lady, gave her another little hug, and said, "It's all right my dear. You'll be President one day if it's over everyone's dead body including him!" They all laughed and The Prez's ball fell off his tee as they then convulsed! The "Don, Don" continued as their laughter waned, "You'll be President, if I have anything to say about it!" And at that precise moment, The First Lady saw an opening that she had been waiting for, for a decade. The First Lady's wheels began to spin, and she was calculating her plan with the skill of a matador. She and Billy Baruhooo had talked about this many, many times before. "HEY! Let's play golf!" The "Don, Don" exhorted! Then he nodded at his favorite blonde of the moment. She knew that she had gained serious brownie points. The "Don, Don" concluded, "Thanks Monica.":o

THE 19ᵀᴴ HOLE BAR AT DORAL

They finished their golf and headed to the bar. The Don, Don" did not drink. He had his reasons. Mostly, the back and of his Mother Dearest. The Prez and The First Lady needed couple. The Prez would have an Arnold Palmer because he laimed it was really a health drink, and The First Lady had a Boilermaker. Coal Country from waaaaaaayyyyyyyyyyy back! Gotta love her.

The bar was vacant. The "Don, Don" always cleared out he bar whenever he had important guests. He once did it on New Year's Eve. It must have cost him $1,000,000 with the bar was closed for 2 hours. "So what!" thought The "Don, Don", "I own the fucking place don't I!?" The Prez, The First Lady and the "Don, Don" all sat down to relax and chat.

"And so the conversation turned..... And then the sun went down.... And many fantasies were learned ..... On that day..." The lyrics bounced around the empty room and The "Don, Don" loved his bad 1970's and 1980's music. What next? Muskrat Love?

They were feeling fascination as the round table of sociopathy would have enthralled Freud. This was a pow wow of narcissism. Probably Mao, Stalin and Hitler would have topped it, but that never occurred. Maybe Jamie Dimon, Lloyd Blankfein and Warren Buffet would be a match? But on sheer cannolis... The First Lady's inclusion in this threesome gave it the win by three lengths. Never met a woman like her. Carly Fiorina? Fahgetaboutit!

So as The Prez gazed at the hottie's outside at the pool, and they knew he was watching as they flashed their tits at him, The "Don, Don" and The First Lady got down to brass tacks. The

First Lady spoke first. It was a critical first foray. It would determine if the master plan was even possible. She said to The "Don, Don", "I'm really going to need you when I run for Senate again from NY." The "Don, Don" nodded. The 1st Lady kept on, "I'm not very well like in too many places because I didn't dump Billy Big Dick over there." The Prez was motioning for the pool girls' attention. They both rolled their eyes at him. The First Lady spoke, "In fact, my favorables are so low, that I need to always run against someone hated even more than myself." "That's the only way I can win," she finished. The "Don, Don" immediately jumped, "Absolutely, Fabulous, I'll raise millions for you. I love you. You know that!" The First Lady tapped The Prez on the arm. He knew he was up to bat with her now. She had just laid the hook in the fish's mouth. She spoke as The Prez focused his attention back on them both. They all three looked at each other. "But we are really going to need you even more when I run for President!" The First Lady noted. At that precise moment, The Prez slowly nodded his head up and down. The "Don, Don" flew up in the air as if Cupid himself had shot him square in his ass. "I AM IN ABSOLUTE LOVE WITH THAT IDEA! FABULOUS, AWESOME, TERRIFIC, AND YOU KNOW I MEAN IT!" The "Don, Don" was in ecstasy! How can I help? How? It was all he kept saying.

THE DOUBLE CROSS

What happened next, well in certain circles they say, the greatest political deal in the History of America transpired that day. Oh this deal is up there with The Manhattan Island Sale, or the Babe Ruth trade. But it was not one-sided. Maybe two faced? The Kennedy Assassination was the greatest hoax ever pulled on the American People ~ and that is verbatim from Nixon. Look it up. This one here was big, but not that big. And are we really talking JFK, RFK, MLK, and Malcom X or all of the above?

The FDR and Wendell Willkie Scam does come to mind here. That was the deal that again delivered the White House to a rather unfavorable FDR looking for a Third Term. This one is probably much more like that one here. You see, without Willkie, FDR may have never led us into WWII. It went a lot like this....

You see. First, FDR approached Willkie ~ a successful businessman. FDR asked Willkie about running against him for President. Willkie was a Democrat who could switch parties in a flash and challenge the President... as a Republican.

Hmmmmm... sounds familiar. But in reality in 1940, Willkie cut a sweet deal with FDR. The crux of the deal was one key issue. Willkie agreed that he would publicly support The Registering of The Military Draft of US Men into the Armed Service as Hitler and Nazism loomed on the horizon of Europe. Not draft them per se, just register the men. Counter to that, FDR would publicly go against it. An Isolationist America, the number one concern of Americans at the moment, would be to vote for FDR in droves! And therefore, Willkie would lose badly because America was very much for peace at the time. As the payoff to the deal, Willkie made a fortune, and FDR made him his

"unofficial/official" roving ambassador to England and Ireland.

Willkie returned home a hero, made tremendous financial deals

in Europe and he was anointed a "partner position" on the

nameplate of a very famous law firm in NYC. Willkie would have

tons of money, tons of power and wouldn't have to do the job as

The President. He supported Roosevelt before this all started,

and he never wanted the job in the first place. That's called The

Art of The Deal...........

"That's what we'll do," smiled The First Lady, "You piss

eeeeeeevrybody off in the world, and you become an

international sensation, you make a fortune in defeat, you get

power, and prestige and we all win! The "Don, Don" with little

hesitation nearly jumped off the table! "It is FANTASTIC! You'll

LOVE it!" [Sociopaths can't differentiate from their ideas and

others ~ it is always their idea] He thundered his approval!

"When do we do it?" The "Don, Don" shouted! He would

become the most famous American in the History of America... in defeat no less! He would become beloved by all the 1% and the true people of the American Silent Majority of the Nixon Days.

He was beside himself. HIS EGO WAS RUNNING WIIIIIILLLLLDDDDDDD!!!!! OH SOCIOPATHS LOVE ATTENTION! The First Lady and The Prez smiled in happiness.

And now the plan......

OUT FAUXED

The First Lady reached for a napkin, and The Prez pulled out a pen, and the scribbling began. To think that Reaganomics and the Laffer Curve were put into motion on just such a napkin sends a chill down my spine. It's like framing a military battle on an Etch-a-sketch. Almost as idiotic as to actually run The "Don, Don" for President.

"Look," said the First Lady, "Edward Snowden and Julian Assange proved one thing. It is that the NSA now knows more about us then we know ourselves. They know how much we own, how much sweetener we take in our coffee in the morning and how we think with these brain games they challenge us to play on line and our smart phones. And they know how to hack into any countries intelligence services." She continued, "For centuries, we have been leaking information about our foreign policy intentions to the world, our friends and our enemies because it keeps them calm and not on edge. Its spy v. spy from the Mad Magazine days. It takes the edge off everyone and the missile silos stay obsolete. Of course we will need to spend TRILLIONS on new systems, and that's how our economy of $2,000,000,000,000 keeps humming along." The "Don, Don" was stymied. He said, "Snowman?" The Prez shook his head, "No, no, my New York State of Mind Friend. He's the guy who leaked that The National Security Agency is evaluating every piece of information in our lives ~ usually by Facebook now, our cameras on our phones and computers, our wired in alarm clocks, home security systems and cameras at McDonalds, everything, and he leaked it to the world!" He continued, "How do you think The First Lady catches me eating hamburgers!?"

The "Don, Don" bellowed with anger! "HE'S A GOD DAMN

TRAITOR!" He continued, "WHO WOULD HAVE CONTACT

WITH THE ENEMY! I WOULD NEVER COLLUDE WITH OUR

ENEMIES LIKE CHINA AND RUSSIA! I HATE PUTIN!" The

First Lady gently tapped him on his forearm, "Yes, Yes my

patriotic friend, but Snowden has been a huge advantage to us.

He opened the door for "we" political types to so intricately data

mine every person in America that we can put together a voting

coalition that is within 100 votes of perfection per congressional

district in all the USA. That my friend is remarkable power.

Anybody who thinks that we think and act freely of monitoring in

this world is behind the times as badly as those Goldwater

Republicans were in 1964…. And I was one of them!" The "Don,

Don" sat in a furious internal rage! He had no idea what the Hell

she was talking about, but he knew there was something to it or

she and The Boy Wonder with their Yale & Georgetown Law

Degrees and Rhodes Scholarships wouldn't be in such a hot and

bothered way. He looked on with contemptuous interest. He

was waaaaay out of his league intellectually, he knew it, but as a sociopath, he could turn the tables on them at any moment by talking about how much money he had. This, they truly believe. "How dare she keep you from eating hamburgers!?" The "Don, Don" yelled!

The First Lady continued, "See, as far back as Carville and Begala getting The Prez here elected, the data mining has grown until this point in time when your buddy Barack has perfected it with Axelrod and his computer geeks who glean the information from the mines of data we now possess via Snowden's leak. Do you know that Obama spent nearly $200,000,000 on data mining alone in figuring out how to defeat Mitt Romney last time around?" The "Don, Don" put his nose in the air, and he raised his sociopathic eyebrows and blurted out, "I HATE THAT SONUVABITCH OBAMA." The Prez rallied, "Yeah, we weren't too fond of him either, but when he showed us the numbers in 2008 after he secured the nomination, we understood that there was a technology out there that could prove out statistically how to win an election and nearly 90% of the American People wouldn't understand it." He continued, "This knowledge would be kept from them with The Mockingbird controlling the media." The "Don, Don" interjected, "I ONLY WATCH FOX NEWS THESE DAYS, BUT THEY ARE STILL SO BLATANTLY RACIST AND BIGOTED." The Prez confided with him as The First Lady looked on, "I know, I know, but they are with us on all of this. Even Putin plays ball with us. But he has that evil KGB streak in him. He can be mitigated with an oil price drop in a heartbeat. It controls the Russian Economy. Look at Venezuela. We, The USA, did that to them with a world oil price drop, and do you think they know what the Hell is going on? Hell, they'll hate socialism forever after this economic crisis. Chavez had to be poisoned with cancer. He was doing too well with socialism. And we finally poisoned Castro too. His brother had no problem helping. Devilish bastard." The "Don, Don (DD)" was shocked, "You mean all that New World Order shit is real?" The First Lady spoke, "Yes, my dearest friend, and a helluva lot more. The growing population in the world is going to challenge us technologically and even at the barest of bones in terms of feeding people. But as we talk about calculating to perfection how to win an election for President, we are also talking about feeding the world and ending human suffering forever." The DD smiled, "We are all Liberals at this table. I believe you as religiously as anyone would or even David Rockefeller." The First Lady smiled again, "Let me give you more."

The First Lady spelled it out, "We are going to change America and the world by first destroying the hate and bigotry that causes The USA to stagnate. The rest of the world moves forward on us, and we still have racial strife, domestic religious wars, male/female fighting in the corporate boardrooms, which you see regularly, not to mention The South is still mired in hating the fact that they lost The Civil War. All these ethnic rivalries are stirred up by The Media and Operation Mockingbird to keep the aggressive American nature feeding our capitalistic dreams. And it perfectly divides the people below the 1%. They fight each other. Not us. But the world is changing. We now need to do good! We need to help our fellow man. Capitalism is always going to be alive and well in the USA and the world. We just don't have to devour ourselves over every morsel of meat on the plate." The DD again wondered how a bird, this damn Mockingbird that they keep mentioning, could influence the entire USA, but he thought maybe it was Avian Flu. The Prez jumped in, "It's divide and conquer, my friend. It always has been. In 2016, we are going to run candidates from every party and faction of the electorate to give everyone out there a chance to vent their emotions and thoughts. The American National Election Cycle will be in full bloom and pump BILLIONS into our domestic economy. It's like a stimulus check to us all every four years. The markets will roar upwards. But we already know how it's going to end up. It's going to be me versus an insane right winged Republican. The Republican Party is nearly dead these days. They hang on to 24% of all voters and they are your KKK / racist ~ bigoted types, Christian Fundamentalists and

Corporate Sociopath Czars. And that's it. Fox and Rupert did a great job cornering them in their bigotry. And he made a ton of money on them too. But eventually, they all die out. Independents are mostly all disgusted Republicans that overwhelmingly go to the Democratic side of the ledger come election time. If the Republicans didn't gerrymander all those states the Republicans would have been dead 20 years ago. The numbers just don't lie. That's how Barack won in 2008 and 2012. Hell, he carried Indiana in 2008! That's the home of the Original Klan!" "I HATE THAT MAN. He embarrassed me in front of all those people in DC when I visited there," spoke the DD. The First Lady looked chagrined, "I'm sorry my friend. We should have told you. He had to do that. It was to set up the racial divide and bring the bigots and racists out of the wood work to follow you or somebody like you. The Mockingbird needed that Media public perception to come out of Black versus White. It is the reason we are here talking to you today.... About you running for President with me!"

The cat jumped squarely out of the bag and landed on The DD's lap! "WHAT THE HELL IS THIS BIRD GOT TO DO WITH ANYTHING?" THE DD BELLOWED! "Please, please understand my friend," spoke The Prez, "We couldn't let you in on everything" until now. It was all need to know as we gleaned information from the data mines. We have the answer to getting Hillary into office, but we need your help."

In great dismay, The "Don, Don" spoke disgustedly, "If you think I'm going to run to be President, you both are out of your minds! I love money! Deals! Hotties! And I have more Power than anyone! I don't need those missile codes. Hell, they don't even work. And this ISIS crap is just bull shit. They couldn't fight their way out of The Bronx!"

The Prez and First Lady both wore a frown. The "Don, Don" could see that he disappointed them, and he needed to save his ass with them if he ever needed a Federal Easement or

Contract in the World anytime soon! He gulped down...... he smiled begrudgingly and said, "Ok, Ok, Ok, if I can help you by running then I will." Ever the crook, he continued, "I'll send you a list of things I want. Make Barack give it to me. That'll fix him! After you get to be President, First Lady, we'll be all squared up if he gives the stuff to me. I'm going to just love being a movie star on the campaign trail! And you know I'm not going to leave the race until the end no matter what."

The Prez spoke, "You are not going to lose. Our PR guys have slogans and comments for you to make that will send your poll numbers soaring. You are going to wake up the echoes from everybody from Nixon, George Wallace to Jefferson Davis and Norman Vincent Peale!" The DD said, "Who? Pele! He was a friendly guy. Met him with the Cosmos years ago." The First Lady rolled her eyes, "It works like this for you. You will annihilate every candidate against you on the Republican side and you will splinter the Republicans into oblivion. Those who know our plan will slowly let the other candidates know what is happening, and they will slowly drop out. The Conservative movement will be told last. Bush, Cruz, Kasich.... The Conservative Movement will be isolated into obscurity and Fox News and This OAN News will be playing their race baiting hate to a fixed number of viewers that will gradually all die out on them. The young members of The Conservative Movement will have no base of support from The Evangelicals nor the Bigots after 2016 to mount a fight against us. The political spectrum in the USA is going to be Capitalistic and Socialistic at the same time. No more D's or R's. That will only be used for the political drama to watch on the tube. It'll be like watching "Suits"! A soap opera for bigots! The American little guy will be transformed from hating each other into working together! Tommy and Sally American are going to get a great deal more to live on. Free health care, low mortgages for homes, free college tuition, lower electric bills... and in short, the corporations are going to get better economic playing fields to make outrageous profits around the world. All because the US Government is going to give them the advantages they need while the common people will get more by enjoying their guaranteed wealth... and ALL because the US Government will guarantee their wealth! It's The New World Order and we're running the whole game! Multinational corporations will always be able to rely on The US of A because do you think the Chinese will protect them? Hell no!" The Prez softly stepped in, "Here is the step by step to making a one party country!"

2016 Presidential Election

"The first, but most important step that you must agree upon is this one matter," said the Prez, "You have to publicly offend EVERYBODY! And I mean everybody, even us! Even your supporters! Conservatives, Gun Owners, even The Vets." The "Don, Don" caught on, "I'll say something about how much I like The Russians and Putin for them!" "YES!" said The Prez, "You got it my friend." The DD asked, "I don't want us to be too rough on each other individually." The Prez said, "We won't. And if it gets too bad or there's a slip, we know it's a mistake.

Real trust between friends here." The DD actually had a tear

come to the side of his eye. He was such a softie. He never

trusted anybody like this in is life.

The Prez continued, "As we slowly let everybody in on the

plan, the anger will wane. Some people in The Republican and

Democratic Party will attack you. As we bring them on board,

they will fade back. Like the true Blue, HA, true Green "Nadar or

nobody" people. When was the last time they won anything?

They just piss people off. They'll probably get Bernie Sanders to

challenge me! But you must offend all. You need to

ESPECIALLY offend all the people on this list on every televised

show, debate and press conference you can get on to. Call them

names! Make up nicknames for them. That always attracts the

most ardent and hateful people in The Republican Party! You

will be box office bonanza for every network. You may be on TV

more than The President." The Prez wrote down the list.

"First there is Barack," said The Prez writing. "Oh that'll be easy," The DD snorted. The First Lady spoke, "We're gonna have to get you two together privately and patch up this nonsense." The DD nodded his head knowingly, "Yes, it just got out of hand. But if it had to happen, and it helped what we are trying to do here! And it makes me famous... And FURIOUS! Then, boy do I love it!" The DD cackled in narcissistic joy! The First Lady said, "Yeah, we knew that would happen. That's why the Black President versus The White Businessman is the perfect starting point and foil to end the hate and bigotry. It is political isometrics placed in a TV Show like a soap!" The DD spoke, "TV, I know that medium well!" The Prez went on, "On the list, there are Women, Hispanics, The Catholics especially the deepest lovers of The Pope, Blacks, LGBTQ, Native Americans, Indians, Asians and Unions. You'll blast "The Press" especially the women at Fox. They are with us. They've been sexually harassed by Roger Ailes for decades! Rupert and his sons want him gone. The boys see the future, and it isn't in racism and stupidity anymore. We help them, they help us. And it will make you look like you are an independent voice from that Republican Biased Network & our good friend Rupert... which of course, you aren't. You need to disgustingly offend everyone on the list. Like your TV Show on Steroids. FIRE THEM ALL! That will do two things. First, it will foment such hate for you that Democrats will come out to vote in mass droves against you in November. And they will vote in the perfect places and states just like our data mining tells us we need big voting turnout. The First Lady's electoral total could reach 400! Second, you'll bring out every looney tune racist and bigot in America. The Evangelicals won't all be too sure of you, and they will probably stay home in their churches on election-day. Only the devoted racists among them will show up! Hell, you might bring back David Duke! That's perfect for us. Less Republican voters the better. The Conservatives like Lindsey Graham and The Bush Family won't help you anywhere. But don't worry. They're in on it with us too. They hate the vile and racist America that they have seen during The Bush and Barack's Presidency. They had to kiss up to the haters to win office, and they hated it. But as we chisel away at the base of

Republican Support, our girl goes up proportionally 1% for every 1% who doesn't vote for you on The Republican side! It works like a charm. Our data mining is more perfect than changing a baby's eye color genetically in the womb these days."

The DD was skeptical, "You mean this will actually work?" The First Lady spoke, "The numbers can't lie. I lost to Barack because of them. Every possible event has been considered and dissected. Even if you don't get the nomination, you will have enflamed so many people on The Left and divided so many people on The Right that I'll win in a walk that way too. If you get the nomination, I'll win in a landslide! And we have a "doomsday machine" that will guarantee everything. All those electronic voting machines… people have fixing elections down to a computer science. With one button at the NSA, 1000 votes can disappear and sway the election in a few counties in the blink of an eye, and that state goes Blue instead of Red. And nobody completely will ever recount an election after Florida in 2000." "Speaking of Red," said The "Don, Don", "WE could even plant a story in the media that accuses our number one enemy in the world has cut a deal with me. That will sway the last remaining vestiges of the white male, patriotic voters to finally disavow me and all the hate I'm gonna spew!" The Prez and The First Lady looked at The DD with absolute surprise! "By George W. I think he's got it!" spoke The First Lady, "And what is with those big words?! Vestiges!??" The DD raised his Mussolini lip in the air, and retorted, "My dear, I went to Penn!" The Prez chimed in, "Don't say much about that below the Mason Dixon line buddy!" They laughed and drank as the Sun set behind them on The Gold Coast. It's always about Gold in the end.

They all laughed with glee. "My dear First Lady," The DD said, "Your victory is Heavenly Music to my ears!" The Prez concluded, "You'll be richer, more famous and more beloved than now on your TV Show! And then on Inauguration day, you will end the hate in America in one swoop of the axe. It may last for a Century when you tell all your racist and bigoted supporters that you have seen the light! And epiphany from God Almighty! You

will tell them that then. You will shout and say and believe that
The Greatest Hope for America Again is a united and successful
Hillary Clinton Presidency! And who isn't going to believe you
after all the outrageous things you'll be changing your mind
about from here on until Inauguration Day. That will be the
silver spike in the heart of the ignorant, stupid, racist and bigoted
America. We must desperately shed them before it's too late!
The Chinese are going to be our most formidable enemy
eventually." They all joined hands in the middle of the table like
Sinatra, Dean and Sammy did in the first "OG" Ocean's Eleven.
A warm smile came to everyone's face. A knowing coup on the
United States had been hatched. It always starts that way. Ask
Allen Dulles.

      In this wonderful state of bliss, The "Don, Don"
interjected, "By the way, what Party am I going to run with?" The
laughter of the jackals was deafening again, "It is going to be
FABULOUS, you know that **and it's going to be the Greatest
Deal that I ever make!**" The threesome raised their glasses

and toasted to victory. "Where's Monica?" The DD sardonically mentioned as he peered out of the side of his eyes at the lady to his left. The First Lady on his left looked at him, "I bet you her name isn't even Monica!" The "Don, Don" smirked, "It isn't." They all roared again! But the First Lady cut The Prez short, "Don't get too brave funny man!" The Prez looked like a deer in the headlights as he immediately stopped laughing.

There were a few more laughs until the Arnold Palmer was just a pool of melted ice in the glass. The goblet had a huge "T" inscribed on its side. What else would it have? They were dancing with the devil in the pale moon light. Thanks to the Joker.

As the titans of the universe walked out of the bar to autograph hounds and shining lights and cameras, The First Lady smiled and said, "I wonder who called these vipers?" The DD smiled with a subtle knowing grin. She spoke again, "Thank you so much." The Prez spoke, "Don't you just love this shit?!"

The "Don, Don" looked at him, "It never gets old my friend. It

never gets old!"

THE SHOW

DONALD TRUMP QUOTES ON THE CAMPAIGN TRAIL

"I could also see Russia being a very big asset to our country."

"Russia, if you're listening, I hope you're able to find the 30,000 emails
that are missing," Trump said at a campaign event in Florida. "I think you
will probably be mightily rewarded by our press."

~

"I call her 'Crooked Hillary' because she's crooked, and you

know the only thing she's got is the woman card," he said.

"That's all she's got, and it is pandering. It's a weak card in

her hands. In another person's hands it could be a powerful

card. I'd love to see a woman president, but she's the wrong

person."

~

"When Mexico sends its people, they're not sending the best. They're not sending you … they're sending people that have lots of problems and they're bringing those problems with us. They're bringing drugs. They're bring crime. They're rapists. And some, I assume, are good people." ~

"I think they're trouble. I think they're looking for trouble," (BLACK LIVES MATTER)

- "Robert Pattinson should not take back Kristen Stewart. She cheated on him like a dog & will do it again – just watch. He can do much better!"

- Megyn Kelly: "You've called women you don't like 'fat pigs,' 'dogs,' 'slobs' and 'disgusting animals.'"

    Trump: "Only Rosie O'Donnell."

- Mocking a disabled journalist

- "We will have so much winning if I get elected that you may get bored with winning."

- "Blood was coming out of her everywhere..." referring to Fox Anchor Megyn Kelly

- "I could stand in the middle of 5th Avenue and shoot somebody, and I wouldn't lose voters."

- "They can go Fuck themselves"- Trump at NH Rally

- "The point is, you can never be too greedy"

- "My IQ is one of the highest – and you all know it. Please don't feel stupid or insecure; it's not your fault."

- "The Wetback Wall"

- "My fingers are long and beautiful, as, it has been well documented, are various other parts of my body. Don't doubt it."

- "I think the only difference between me and the other candidates is that I'm honest and my women are more beautiful."

- "Back in the old days (these protestors) wouldn't get out of here."

- "The beauty of me is that I'm rich."

- "I've said if my daughter wasn't my daughter that I would probably be dating her."

- "You know, it really doesn't matter what (the media) writes as long as you've got a young and beautiful piece of ass."

- "It's like in golf. A lot of people — I don't want this to sound trivial — but a lot of people are switching to these really long putters, very unattractive. It's weird. You see these great players with these really long putters because they can't sink three-footers anymore. And I hate it. I am a traditionalist. I have so many fabulous friends who happen to be gay, but I am a traditionalist."

"Many times it appears to me,

that those God intends to destroy;

He first gives money...."

www.ingramcontent.com/pod-product-compliance
Lightning Source LLC
Chambersburg PA
CBHW060648290526
45793CB00001B/441